A WEEK in the Life

*Understanding the Role of a
Project Manager*

Janice Y. Rodgers, PMP
&
Brenda K. Williams, PMP

ISBN:1495925994
ISBN-13:978-1495925993

DEDICATION

This book is dedicated to our families and friends who have been patient with us and helped us as we worked through various book ideas and concepts.

*Special thanks to our husbands (Rick and Roman) for ALWAYS being there to support us.

We love you!

Janice & Brenda

Table of Contents

FOREWORD

Project management is an art as much as it is a science. It lends itself to foundation and principles, yet leaves room for ingenuity and flair. Both art and science are repeatable based on a reference point and project management is the same. If you are anything like me, you basically know what needs to be done and you usually have a general idea of how to get there.

This book, *A Week in the Life: Understanding the Role of a Project Manager,* helps you quickly understand the foundational components of a project, the project manager's role, and then gives you a solid starting point. It provides a much needed day-by-day project guide to take you through each major planning area, and includes the meetings needed, who should attend, and agendas. Perhaps your project is not mature enough to require a rigorous first week. No problem: pick and choose based on your project needs and experience. This book is meant to be a guide, not the gospel. Remember, "art *and* science"—there is more than one way (or more than one journey) to the result.

A Week in the Life: Understanding the Role of a Project Manager allows you to find what you need quickly and then use your experience to fill in the rest. It's almost like painting by numbers; you have a great reference, as well as guidance and room for flair and finesse. You can start anywhere you like, based on where you are in your project. The end result is the same—a successful project, and no one knows where you started, only where you ended up.

Lakesia M. Campbell, PMP

Association of Women in Computing – President 2010-11

i

Introduction

Have you ever wanted to pick up a project management book that you could quickly understand? One that contained relevant business terminology, and actually took you through a "week in the life" of a project manager? Then look no further! You have found a great reference that takes you through a real-world business scenario and allows you to sit on the sidelines as a project manager begins a project. This book allows you to understand where a project manager fits in, how they plan, how they work with various groups in the company, and how they make an impact in planning and delivering a successful project.

The business scenario aka "the project" used in the book is for a multinational company as they start on a Customer Relationship Management (CRM) pilot. You will learn how to apply the basic tenets of the Project Management Institute® (PMI) methodology (the foundation) in a real-world situation using our key project management elements (stepping stones) we've termed "project PASTELS."

The "PASTELS" acronym is an easy way to understand and remember the key components of a project.

- The **P** in PASTELS stands for the importance of planning *the people* and *priorities* of a project.
- The **A** stands for the need to understand *action items, accountability* and *risk*.
- The **S** stands for the *scope* and *status* of the project.
- The **T** stands for the *timelines* and *templates* needed to ensure your project stays on track.
- The **E** stands for *expenses, effort* and *procurement* to manage the project.
- The **L** stands for *leadership* and *communication* needed on every project.
- The **S** is for *success*, which represents the integration of all components and the quality of them.

As you can see in Figure 1, these project PASTELS form seven cornerstones of project management every project should incorporate.

Project Management Approach

Project PASTELS

Figure 1: Project Management Approach - Project PASTELS

How this Book is Organized

To help you get the most out of this book, the information within it is arranged in two parts:

- Part One - The Foundation. The first part of the book focuses on providing context and explains the foundational elements of project execution. It includes details on the business scenario presented in the book and also includes the basics on how to create and conduct a meeting.

  Scenario: the scenario provides details on the company that will be implementing the pilot project. It gives you basic contextual information you need to understand why the company is willing to embark on a pilot CRM project, and the departments that need to be involved in the process.

  Meeting Basics (Quick Tips): the meeting basics section describes how to organize meetings. This key skill is fundamental to all projects. There will be many planning meetings, status meetings, design meetings, development meetings, deployment meetings, budget meetings, and so on. Meetings move the team forward successfully, and help attain the objectives of the project. Fundamental to any successful project is to understand how to start, conduct, end, and follow up on meetings.

- Part Two - The Project Stepping Stones. The second part of the book focuses on breaking down the seven key elements or cornerstones of project management. These cornerstones are presented through the PASTELS acronym and are specific to each chapter.

Chapter Sections: The chapters cover the project PASTELS by introducing key meetings or steps that are important to help ensure a successful project.

Understanding and applying these PASTELS through these meetings are important to quickly and succinctly define the project's purpose, plan the project effectively, and kick off the project. The PASTELS enable easy application of basic project management principles, to help ensure the project is planned and implemented appropriately each time.

Part 1: The Foundation

The Scenario

JB Hair Care, LLC (JBH) is a multinational company with distribution channels worldwide. JBH specializes in hair products to improve growth and sustain healthy hair production.

The sole mission of JBH is to help customers grow hair one strand at a time. JBH started in 1965 in Chicago, Illinois, out of the house of the founders: sisters Janice and Brenda Sagwa. Janice and Brenda saw their father and grandfather struggle with losing their hair early, and were committed to helping all people (men and women) find a hair-growth regimen that could be designed and personalized for each person.

JBH started with one small office in Chicago, and then quickly grew by 1975 to 25 offices throughout the United States. In 1975, JBH made the corporate decision to go multinational, and began distributing their products to Japan and India. Today, JBH has grown to 40 offices in the United States and ten offices throughout Europe, with over $15B in sales.

Issue

JBH is currently expanding and needs to upgrade their systems to meet the continuous demand for their products. The project at hand is to develop and deliver a Customer Relationship Management (CRM) system to keep track of the sales pipeline, as well as understand the needs of over 20,000 sales representatives.

A Week in the Life is a depiction of the first week of the project. Figure 2 is a graphical representation of that week from the project management perspective.

Remember, even though these meetings are presented within a scheduled week, they can be expanded over a month or longer depending on the size, scope, and complexity of the project.

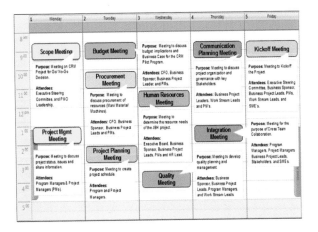

Figure 2: JBH Project Management Week-in-the-Life

Schedule Breakdown

Monday

begins the week, and the project, with an 8:30 a.m. meeting to discuss the scope of the Customer Relationship Management (CRM) pilot project. This is the first meeting of the week, and it focuses on the S (scope) in the PASTELS elements. (Before a project can really begin, the scope must be discussed and defined.) On this project, the project authorization request has been reviewed, and it is the task of executive leadership to review the final draft of the project charter and approve or disapprove the draft with the project management office (PMO) leadership. In this instance, the executive leadership has given their approval to proceed with the scope as stated. See "Chapter 1: Scope Meeting" for more details.

At 1:00 p.m., the PMO gathers the project managers who will be instrumental in the project initiative. The initial purpose of this meeting is to assign project management resources to the project and explain the objective of the project. For this use, the meeting focuses on the S (scope/status) in the PASTELS elements. On a recurring basis, this meeting will be beneficial to discuss project status and issues, and to share planning information across the project management team. This meeting will help to ensure communication is open, and progress is tracked consistently and appropriately. See "Chapter 6: Integration/Planning Meeting" for more details.

Tuesday

starts off at 8:30 a.m., focusing on the budget of the project. This is a very important meeting, because it outlines how much money will be invested and addresses the E (expenses) in the PASTELS elements. This meeting discusses budget implications and the business case for the Customer Relationship Management pilot program. The Chief Financial Officer (CFO), the business sponsor, the business project leader, and program manager will all be in attendance. See "Chapter 2: Budget Meeting" for more details.

At 10:00 a.m., the project leaders convene for the procurement meeting. This meeting focuses on procurement of resources (services), hardware, and software for the CRM pilot program. The CFO, business sponsor, business project leader, and program manager, will all be in attendance. The procurement meeting is also covered under the E (expenses) in the PASTELS elements. See "Chapter 5: Procurement Meeting" for more details.

At 2:00 p.m., the project managers will meet to create the project schedule/work plan. This meeting is led by the program manager. The project managers for each of the work streams should be in attendance. This meeting enables coordination between the work streams and allows the schedules to roll up to the program level. This meeting works to integrate all the elements of the project, and it focuses on the T (timeline) in the PASTELS elements. Without timelines and planning, the Customer Relationship Management (CRM) project cannot be successful. See "Chapter 6: Integration/Planning Meeting" for more details on the schedule/work plan.

Wednesday

focuses on determining the resource needs of the project. Now that the scope, budget, and initial planning meetings have been conducted, it is time to detail the specific people needed, which represents the P (people) in the PASTELS elements. The human resource meeting, held at 11:00 a.m., accomplishes this by discussing resource availability, skillsets needed, time commitments, schedules, and locations for the Customer Relationship Management pilot program. The executive steering committee (which includes all executive-level management), the HR (Human Resources) lead, the business sponsor, the business project leader, and the program manager, will all be in attendance. See "Chapter 3: Human Resources Meeting" for more details.

At 3:30 p.m., the project leadership will meet to develop the quality planning and management. This meeting is led by the business sponsor. The business project leader, the program manager/project managers, as well as the work stream lead for each of the work streams, should be in attendance. This meeting enables coordination on appropriate quality standards and procedures to be executed throughout the project. This meeting focuses on the S (success) in the PASTELS elements, because it works to integrate many project components and test the quality of the resulting products. See "Chapter 7: Quality Meeting" for more details.

Thursday

starts off at 8:30 a.m., focusing on the communication needs of the project. This meeting reviews and refines the project organization, as well as develops program governance (i.e., issues, risks, change requests, and action items) for the Customer Relationship Management pilot program. This meeting focuses on the L (leadership) in the PASTELS elements, and the meeting's goal is to help with project communication throughout the work streams. It looks at each piece of the project and describes how each element in the project will communicate and what it will share. The PMO resources (program manager and project managers), the business project leader, and the work stream leads, will be in attendance. See "Chapter 4: Communications Meeting" for more details.

At 1:00 p.m., the project leaders convene for the Integration/Planning Meeting. This meeting focuses on cross-team collaboration for the Customer Relationship Management (CRM) pilot program. It addresses both the S (success) and the T (timelines) elements of the project PASTELS. It combines overall integration planning with project timeline or schedule planning. The business project leader, program manager, project managers, stakeholders, and subject matter experts (SME) will all be in attendance. See "Chapter 6: Integration/Planning Meeting" for more details.

Friday

focuses on kicking off the project. The 8:30 a.m. kickoff meeting discusses project purpose, project organization, high-level timelines, roles and responsibilities, and next steps for the CRM pilot program. This meeting addresses the S (success) in the PASTELS elements, because the meeting works to help with overall project success and supports key team communication and integration. The executive steering committee, the business sponsor, the business project leader, the program manager, the project managers, the work stream leads, and SMEs, will all be in attendance. See "Chapter 8: Kickoff Meeting" for more details.

Meeting Basics (Quick Tips)

One of the most important communication tools that organizations like to use, and sometimes misuse, is a meeting. A meeting is a simple tool, used to quickly and clearly communicate ideas, status, and actions to move projects through the project lifecycle. However, if not managed correctly, meetings can spiral out of control, often not accomplishing anything.

For example, have you ever been in those meetings where at the end you actually wondered what the meeting was about in the first place? This Meeting Basics (Quick Tips) section will provide you with a few key, foundational pointers to plan, manage, and execute your meetings. This ensures your meetings are on task and produce the results you need to help manage and implement your projects.

Pre-Meeting Checklist

Okay, let's start at the beginning. Let's plan the meeting. I know this is a seldom practiced habit, but one that can pay numerous dividends. The first thing to do is ask yourself, *What's the purpose of the meeting?* This is critically important, because you need to write down *why* you want to have the meeting and then most importantly, *your expected results.* This will keep everyone at the meeting (including you) stay laser focused on the outcome and on achieving it. This also helps to focus people in the meeting who might want to introduce other topics—in the project management world, we call them "meeting hijackers."

To retain your intended purpose, create an agenda that will be appropriate for the amount of time you have outlined for the meeting and the subject matter. In Figure 3, you will find the example of an agenda template that can help you plan your meeting. This example is for the JBH Communications Meeting, which focuses on project organization and governance with key team stakeholders.

JBH Communication Meeting Agenda				
Date: 01/10/20XX				
Time: 08:30 AM				
Place: Conference Room - Platinum				
Attendees				
Sema West	Drey Alexander	Kim Sullivan	Felix Dunlevy	Sylvia Duncan
Trudy Arnold	Iris Faulkner	Iris Faulkner		

Agenda		
Timeframe	**Agenda Item**	**Named Resource**
8:30	Communications Process Review	
9:00	Communications Matrix Review	
9:15	Next Steps	

Discussion Topics	Notes and Key Decisions

Action Items	Responsible For Follow-up	Due Date	Status

Issues / Change Requests / Risks	Responsible To Log	Due Date

Figure 3: JBH Project Meeting Agenda

After you've identified your purpose (objective), expected results and agenda, brainstorm on identifying all the people who need to attend your meeting to achieve your expected results. To do this, you should create a roles-and-responsibilities list that clearly identifies each role on the project, as well as in the specific meeting. As an example, the JBH project team's responsibilities list can be found in Figure 4.

Project Team - Responsibilities

Business Sponsor (Project Owner)	• Provide financial funding for the program • Provide project support and alignment to strategic directions • Collaborate with Change Review Board to support change management processes
Change Control Board (CCB)	• Provide support and guidance for all changes to project scope • Identify tools and techniques used to standardize the process • Approve/ Decline Program Changes
Project Office (Coordination/Support)	• Provide support and guidance to project managers • Identify tools and techniques used to standardize the process • Provide dashboard/status reporting
Business Project Leader	• Provide support and guidance to work stream • Identify Subject Matter Experts (SMEs) • Identify and escalate issues • Ensure alignment of process and business
Team Members (All Work Streams)	• Provide input to weekly status updates • Identify and document issues, action items, change requests, risks, key decisions • Demonstrate project support by communicating buy-in and understanding of project benefits to stakeholders and end users
SME's (Provide Accuracy)	• Represent functional areas by participating in assigned workshops/ sessions, scheduled meetings, webinars, training session • Advise on and validate work stream activities • Provide input/feedback on change impacts • Provide guidance on respective work stream processes • Communicate work stream requirements

Figure 4: JBH Project Team Roles & Responsibilities

This responsibilities list illustrates the roles in the JBH project, and is used to clearly identify who should be at the meeting and why (based on the topic of discussion).

Here's the tricky part, and often the part overlooked: If you are dealing with a complicated topic, or even think the topic needs to be thoroughly understood before your meeting, it is a good idea to have a pre-meeting with select attendees. This helps to ensure you can address important, complicated issues prior to the meeting and obtain a level of consensus. This also helps your primary meeting retain its focus on key topics as opposed to peripheral issues.

After your pre-meeting is complete and your vital attendees understand the upcoming meeting's expectations, now it's time to identify a date that will work. Best practice is to ensure you coordinate schedules with the senior players or VIPs (decision makers) who will be attending your meeting. These are the people you need to attend, to ensure the expected results of the meeting. All other attendees need to adjust their schedules to the senior/VIPs' (the decision makers) schedules. When you do finally send out the invitation, ensure you have given up to two weeks' notice, if possible, to allow time for attendees to make their schedules accommodate the meeting.

The next few tasks are administrative preparation for the meeting. Secure a room, and a projector (if needed); arrange for a call-in number and/or video conference equipment in case you have attendees who are remote; verify the roles and responsibilities of the people who will help facilitate the meeting; then prepare the final meeting documents.

Once all of these items are complete—at least a week before the meeting—it's time to send out an update to your initial invite. This update will include the meeting agenda, the meeting's objective(s) and expected results, and any meeting documents you would like your attendees to review before the meeting. Sometimes this is called "pre-work."

Once these items have been taken care of, you have successfully planned a meeting.

The easy-to-use pre-meeting checklist below can help you track and check off the required steps.

Pre-Meeting Checklist

- ☐ Identify Purpose
- ☐ Identify Expected Results
- ☐ Identify Ground Rules
- ☐ Develop the Agenda—Use Agenda Template (See Figure 3)
- ☐ Develop Attendees List—Use Company Organization Chart (See Figure 7)
- ☐ Conduct a Pre-Meeting (if needed)
- ☐ Identify Date of the Meeting—Use Company Calendar
- ☐ Time—Start and End of Meeting (meeting duration—make sure this is appropriate for your subject matter)
- ☐ Identify Roles/Responsibilities for Attendees— Roles/Responsibilities List (See Figure 4)
- ☐ Prepare Materials for Presentation

- ☐ Schedule a Meeting Room
- ☐ Obtain a conference call number or video equipment if needed
- ☐ Order food/snacks (Meetings held between 11:30 – 1:00 should provide lunch or at the very least inform the attendees to get lunch before the meeting)
- ☐ Send Meeting Invite (as well as all necessary documents) with Meeting Room location identified

Conduct Meeting Checklist

Congratulations, you have planned your meeting! Now it's time to actually conduct it. Keep in mind, if you don't conduct the meeting correctly, your best-laid plans will mean nothing to moving the project forward. Planning and conducting a meeting in a coordinated, organized manner is the true key to its success. The following five steps clearly articulate how to execute a successful meeting:

1. Identify who is in attendance. It's a good idea to send around a sign-in sheet and do a roll-call introduction (include people on the conference call if applicable). The sign-in sheet should include all invitees, with blanks at the end for any last-minute attendees. Include a column for contact information, including name, e-mail address, phone/extension, and team. This step allows you to assess from the beginning if you have the right people in the meeting and can conduct it successfully. It also enables you to follow up the meeting appropriately, with minutes and action items. Also, if you are facilitating the meeting, make sure you have a designated scribe to document meeting discussions, activities and follow-up.

2. Once you've established that you have the right players in the room (and on the phone if needed), open the meeting and introduce yourself. There have been many meetings where project managers/ managers have opened the meeting with the assumption that everyone knew who they were, and

they were sometimes incorrect.

3. After you introduce yourself, discuss the administrative items and the ground rules. After everyone is clear on how to conduct themselves in the meeting, have everyone else introduce themselves and their respective roles. After introductions are complete, make sure everyone has the meeting materials, then review the agenda and work through and discuss each topic appropriately.

4. At the end of the meeting, it is very important to summarize the meeting outcomes and then discuss next steps. Ensure that any questions or issues that come up are addressed either in the conversation or in an action item/parking lot. Ensure you do not forget about the remote attendees on the phone. Constantly include them, and make sure they know where you are in the agenda and presentation material.

5. Overall, the attendees should leave with a good understanding of what they accomplished and how to move the objective to the next step. The meeting should be closed with thanking everyone for their attendance and their time, and to expect an e-mail from you, one that summarizes the key points of the meeting (minutes) and gives the next steps. It is also wise to remind everyone to follow up on his or her respective action items, and provide a status update to the project manager.

It goes without saying, but it's so important, this is worth repeating: You MUST start the meeting on time and end the meeting on time, pass out your agenda and other materials, and collect any extra materials at the end of the meeting (for cleanup/confidentiality). This ensures a properly organized meeting, and almost guarantees people will attend a meeting conducted by you in the future!

Conduct-Meeting Checklist

- ☐ Distribute Sign-In Sheet
- ☐ Open Meeting and Introduce Yourself
- ☐ Administrative Items (restroom locations, break times, meeting materials, and so on)
- ☐ Discuss Ground Rules
- ☐ Make Introductions
- ☐ Review Agenda (See Figure 3)
- ☐ Discuss Agenda Topics
- ☐ Capture Action Items, Issues, Risks, Parking Lot Items, Decisions, and Next Steps
- ☐ Summarize Meeting
- ☐ Reiterate Next Steps
- ☐ Close Meeting

Now that you've completed the two most difficult parts of any meeting—planning the meeting and conducting the meeting—you are almost finished! Now it's time to discuss the icing on the cake: the follow-up. Proper follow-up actually helps make sure you stay in the minds of the attendees with follow-up actions; this also makes sure they are delivering on their actions until your next meeting.

First, you will need to consolidate your meeting notes and then socialize them to gain consensus with the attendees or your manager (if needed). Getting approval from your manager is sometimes needed before you send the minutes out. This decision depends on the subject matter of the meeting, your position, and various other factors. You and your manager should discuss and act accordingly.

When you distribute the minutes, include the notes, action items, people assigned, and due date. Make sure to be eco-friendly: Send a link as opposed to e-mailing large attachments; attachments fill up the IT servers quickly and server space is always a valid IT concern.

Your final actions, which pertain to any meeting, are to review your project plan, update it based on the expected outcomes of the meeting, and schedule any follow-up meeting(s). Below is a post-meeting checklist you can use as a quick-tip guide to make sure you have completed all the necessary steps.

Post-Meeting Checklist

- ☐ Consolidate and Socialize Minutes
- ☐ Send Minutes to Attendees
- ☐ Send Action Items to Assignees
- ☐ Send Reminder(s) on Items Due Prior to the Next Meeting
- ☐ Touch Base with Attendees Who have Items Due and Obtain Status
- ☐ Update Project Plan and Other Project Documents with Revisions
- ☐ Schedule Follow-Up Meeting(s)

A meeting is an amazing tool to use, as long as it is used correctly. By applying the simple checklists outlined above, you can easily plan, conduct, and follow up on meetings to help move your project forward and meet the project's objectives. Refer back to these checklists every time you plan a meeting, and they will consistently help you practice good techniques.

Since you now understand how to conduct effective meetings, and have sufficiently built your foundational understanding of the project at hand, it's time to learn about the steps you will need to take to progress the project forward. The project stepping stones are broken down in part 2 of this book by outlining the key meetings using the project PASTELS. Each chapter will focus you on a specific PASTEL and provide a deeper understanding of how these project stepping stones are developed and implemented.

The first chapter, beginning on the following page, introduces the scope meeting. This is the first meeting or stepping stone all projects should take to ensure clarity of purpose and understanding with the project stakeholders.

Part 2: Project Stepping Stones

Chapter 1: Scope Meeting

P urpose: Meet with the executive steering committee to introduce the potential scope of the Customer Relationship Management (CRM) project (in-scope and out-of-scope requirements), risks, and options for a pilot program implementation—GO/NO-GO Decision. This meeting focuses on the S (scope) of the PASTELS project management elements. Scope must be defined first; to make certain everyone on the project team understands the task at hand prior to planning.

Conduct Scope Meeting

To conduct the JBH Scope Meeting, it is first necessary to understand the meaning of scope, and the use of a clearly defined and managed scope throughout the project. Actually, defining scope and continually updating it as appropriate is the most important part of any project.

To effectively execute any project, it is imperative to fully understand and communicate the scope of the project. In this scenario, scope is part of the planning process where the executive steering committee reviews for approval a project's requirements. These requirements are collected and presented as a narrative that defines what is in-scope and out-of-scope.

To have a successful JBH Scope Meeting, the project manager breaks the subject matter into three key areas: requirements, scope, and work breakdown structure. Once the details of the meeting have been presented, the executive steering committee will provide a decision to "go" or "no-go" for project continuation. In our scenario, the decision is a go.

Requirements

Definition: Define and document stakeholder needs to meet the project objectives. (*PMBOK® Guide Fourth Edition*, 2008; page 49)

Stakeholders: The stakeholders invited to the JBH Scope Meeting consist of the executive steering committee. These stakeholders were invited because they approve all major projects over one million dollars, plan and manage the budget of the company, and understand the vision and objectives of the company. Additionally, they are the executives who will either move this project forward, ensuring it meets the company's objectives, or stop the project during critical go/no-go decision milestones.

Requirements: To clearly document the requirements of the JBH Customer Relationship Management (CRM) pilot, several meetings are required to generate and form consensus on the project. The proponents of this system from both the business and IT areas met and developed a detailed justification of the project. They fully understand the needs of the company and the capabilities that a CRM system will provide, including how these capabilities are critical for JBH to grow. These business and technology leads have also completed a high-level business case that breaks down the hard and soft benefits of the project.

Scope

Definition: Create a description of the project and the product, which is detailed in the project charter. (*PMBOK® Guide Fourth Edition*, 2008; page 49).

Process: The process of defining scope for JBH consists of first identifying the needs of the various departments. Going in, it's vital to understand assumptions, clearly articulate expectations on current scope, determine the definition of scope creep for the particular project, and decide the processes to change/update the scope statement within the project charter.

Template: To develop the JBH scope statement, the project manager will fill in the project charter template with key project information including the project name, charter and stakeholders. Also, in the scope statement, there should be a clear project justification, which includes a listing of requirements and the associated project plan milestones and deliverables. Additionally, you need to include high-level cost estimates. Remember to document all items that are clearly outside the scope of your project. This will ensure everyone is clear on what is included and excluded upfront. This document should be updated throughout the project, and distributed to the project team and stakeholders as needed.

Work Breakdown Structure

Definition: A work breakdown structure (WBS) is simply a way to subdivide the project deliverables and project work into smaller, more manageable pieces. (*PMBOK® Guide Fourth Edition*, 2008; page 49). You can think of it as the logical breakdown of work, and how to best organize it, for the people who will be working on the project and the people who are responsible for governance.

Process: The process of creating a work breakdown structure is to first have a clear understanding of scope (via the scope statement in the project charter), then to look at the project's objective (make sure this is clear and commonly understood). The work breakdown structure should show a subdivision of effort required to achieve your objective. When creating a WBS, you start with the end objective in mind and successively subdivide it into manageable components in terms of size, duration and responsibility (e.g., systems, subsystems, components, tasks, subtasks, and work packages).

Template: To develop the JBH work breakdown structure, the project manager will first fill out the work breakdown structure (WBS) template. The template of a WBS consists of an organizational structure. Start at defining the Customer Relationship Management (CRM) pilot as the overall objective, and then decompose the pieces of the project from a project management perspective. You will continue doing this until you have successfully completed the WBS. When you have documented the lowest element of a work package (meaning the cost and schedule of the work can be reliably estimated) you have completed the WBS. See Figure 5 for an example of a work breakdown structure that illustrates a few key elements from a project management perspective.

Figure 5: JBH WBS Example

Chapter 2: Budget Meeting

P urpose: Meet with the CFO to discuss budget and business case implications for the Customer Relationship Management (CRM) pilot program. This meeting focuses on the E (expenses and effort) of the PASTELS project management elements. Project expenses must be analyzed and defined to ensure that appropriate resources are identified for the budget to meet the project objectives.

Conduct Budget Meeting

To conduct the JBH Budget meeting, it is first necessary to understand the components of Project Cost Management (PCM).

Cost management consists of identifying the costs and then developing the budget. The budget is derived from a series of meetings where costs are estimated, and then summarized, to develop an overall budget. Once these costs have been aggregated, this establishes the authorized cost baseline. All expenses for the project should be charged to the established cost baseline (budget). This baseline is key to understanding how each cost affects the budget, and how project burn (how actuals are applied to planned) is defined and established.

Typically, budgets are reviewed on a monthly basis and compared to actuals. Once the variance is identified, mitigation approaches on over or under-budget calculations need to be completed and actions taken to get the project back on track or maintain the project's on-budget status. Reforecasting is also completed on a monthly basis, to make sure the project budget is in line with the project's expected expenses, and is not over or understated.

To effectively conduct this JBH Budget Meeting, the project manager should focus on two key areas: estimating the costs and developing the budget.

Estimate Costs

Definition: Develop an approximation of the monetary resources needed to complete project activities. (*PMBOK® Guide Fourth Edition*, 2008; page 165).

Stakeholders: The stakeholders invited to the JBH Budget meeting consist of the CFO, business sponsor, business project leader, and project managers. These stakeholders were invited because they are the key people involved in approving the budget baseline and associated expenses. This group is also responsible for maintaining overall governance of the project budget.

Requirements: To understand and estimate the costs of the JBH Customer Relationship Management (CRM) pilot program, before this meeting, the proponents of this project from both the financial and project leader organizations met and developed a detailed description of the estimated costs and justification. During this session, the team identified the costing alternatives that focused on decisions of buy vs. build, lease vs. buy, and the sharing of resources to maximize resource utilization.

As the project progresses, the validity of these project estimates will be improved through the process of progressive elaboration. This process is an iterative cycle of reviewing estimates and comparing them to actuals to determine the validity of the estimates. Keep in mind, all costs to the project are estimated (for example: labor, materials, facilities, equipment, services, and other potential costs). Key methods used to derive cost estimates are expert judgment, and bottom up/top down estimating. Expert judgment involves using experts to develop estimates based on past experiences. Bottom up/top down estimating means to start either at the very highest level and estimate, or start at the very lowest level and estimate. The key to estimating is to have a reference point and estimate based on the closest facts you have that make sense. It is truly an art and a science, yet the only key requirement is that it makes sense for your particular situation.

Develop Budget

Definition: Create a cost baseline (program budget) by aggregating the estimated costs. (*PMBOK® Guide Fourth Edition*, 2008; page 165).

Process: The process of defining a budget for the JBH Customer Relationship Management (CRM) pilot program consists of first aggregating all the costs identified per the work breakdown structure (WBS) elements.

After costs are accumulated, a management/contingency reserve is established (usually somewhere between 10 – 15% based on the company policies). These costs must be reviewed against the funding and timing constraints of the project.

The results of aggregating costs and reviewing them against the project funding constraints is the cost performance baseline. This baseline is used to measure, monitor and control overall cost performance on the project. (*PMBOK® Guide Fourth Edition*, 2008; page 178).

Template: To develop the JBH program budget, the project manager will fill in the template with key project information including the project name, project expenses, rate or cost per resource, utilization of resources, cost per month, and the final total and cumulative costs. See Figure 6 for a visual of a high-level program budget.

| JBH Project Budget | Rate Per Day | Program Cost Budget by Month | | | | | | | | | | | Project: CRM Pilot | |
| | | Month 1 | | Month 2 | | Month 3 | | Month 4 | | Month 5 | | Month 6 | |
Labor	Day	#Day	Cost	#Day	Cost	#Day	Cost	#Day	Cost	#Day	Cost	#Day	Cost
Senior Developer	$500	10	$5,000	0	$0	0	$0	0	$0	0	$0	0	$0
Junior Developer	$700	0	$0	0	$0	0	$0	0	$0	0	$0	0	$0
Project Manager	$300	30	$9,000	30	$9,000	30	$9,000	30	$9,000	30	$9,000	30	$9,000
Technical Architect	$400	30	$12,000	5	$2,000	5	$2,000	5	$2,000	5	$2,000	5	$2,000
Information Arch.	$300	30	$9,000	5	$1,500	5	$1,500	5	$1,500	5	$1,500	5	$1,500
DBA	$700	0	$0	30	$2,100	30	$2,100	30	$2,100	30	$2,100	30	$2,100
Labor Subtotal		100	$35,000	70	$14,600	70	$14,600	70	$14,600	70	$14,600	70	$14,600
ERP Software			$0		$0		$0		$0		$0		$0
ERP Consulting			$15,000		$15,000		$2,000		$2,000		$2,000		$2,000
Licensing & Warranty			$6,000		$1,000		$200		$200		$200		$200
H/W & S/W Subtotal			$21,000		$16,000		$2,200		$2,200		$2,200		$2,200
Subtotal			$56,000		$30,600		$16,800		$16,800		$16,800		$16,800
Contingency	10%		$5,600		$3,060		$1,680		$1,680		$1,680		$1,680
Contingency Subtotal			$5,600		$3,060		$1,680		$1,680		$1,680		$1,680
Cost			$61,600		$33,660		$18,480		$18,480		$18,480		$18,480

Figure: 6: JBH Program Budget

As the project realizes actual expenses, these actuals need to be compared to budget, and any over/under-budget needs to be reforecasted. The over-budget items should be brought up to management, along with a plan to resolve the items during future project months. This document should be continually updated and reviewed for appropriate action throughout the project.

Chapter 3: Human Resources Meeting

P urpose: Meet with the executive steering committee to discuss resource availability: skill sets needed, people available, time commitment, schedule, and locations.

This meeting focuses on the P (people & priorities) of the PASTELS project management elements. To create the project team, people with the appropriate skills must be identified and brought on/off the project in a coordinated manner.

Conduct Human Resources Meeting

To conduct the JBH Human Resources (HR) meeting, it is first necessary to understand the components of Project Human Resource Management. Human Resource management consists of identifying the organizational structure, the roles and responsibilities, and the staffing plan. (*PMBOK® Guide Fourth Edition*, 2008; page 218). These elements, placed into their appropriate documents, collectively form the foundation of the Human Resource Plan for the project.

- The organizational structure is a key document, to ensure everyone understands reporting structure, the departments in the project, the key resources, and how each stakeholder and project participant will interact with each other.

- The roles-and-responsibilities document further clarifies the activities performed by role, and presents how the roles interact as they work on the project.

- The staffing plan consists of the activities requested, the skills required to perform those activities, the people available to fill those needs, the timing of when those resources are needed and available, the variances in resources, and the costs associated with supplementing the resources. The initial HR plan is reviewed in this meeting, and further refined through progressive elaboration.

Organizational Structure

Definition: Develop the organizational structure for the project. This includes all project organizations, participants, support teams, steering committees, and governance team members. This ensures all stakeholders are clearly identified, and the structure is properly communicated. See Figure 7 for an example of the JBH Organization Structure.

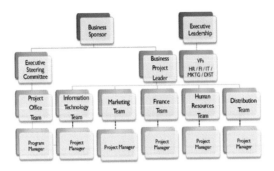

Figure 7: JBH Project Organization Chart

Stakeholders: The stakeholders invited to the JBH HR meeting consist of the executive steering committee, the business sponsor, the business project leader, project manager, and HR work stream lead. These stakeholders were invited because they are the key people involved in understanding the resource requirements for the project, the project's budget, and the overall timing and staffing considerations. This group is also responsible for updating and maintaining this organizational structure.

Requirements: To understand the resources for this project, before this meeting the project manager and HR leadership met and developed a detailed description of the scope of the project, the activities that need to be executed, and the types of people needed (skillsets) to successfully execute this project.

Roles and Responsibilities

Definition: Create a roles-and-responsibilities document that outlines the role for each team member and their relative responsibilities on the project.

Process: The process of defining roles-and-responsibilities is a simple but vitally important activity. This step is crucial in communicating what positions exist as well as how the positions interact with each other. The first step in the process is to review the high-level project plan and identify all the key activities; the second step is to ensure with HR that you have the positions to fulfill those activities; the next step is to further define how those people will work in the project and with whom they will interact. See Figure 4 for an example of the JBH Roles and Responsibilities List.

Staffing Plan

Definition: Create a staffing plan to clearly lay out resource needs, roles, timeframe required on the project, rates, and overall budget impact.

Process: The process of defining a staffing plan for the JBH Customer Relationship Management pilot program consists of first identifying all skillsets needed by specific department, and then identifying the timing in which they are needed. After the types of skills have been identified, it is necessary to understand where these resources will come from. Sources for skilled workers are either through the company's various departments, or by contracting out work for specific areas of the project. With each resource, a cost must be established and the time frame needed (start and end dates).

Template: To develop the JBH staffing plan, the project manager will fill in the template with key activities from the project, the skillsets required, the resource names that have been requested to fill those positions, the start and end dates of the resource, the weeks and hours requested, and the rate or cost of the person/supply/equipment. This information forms a great basis for the initial project budget. This document should be continually updated throughout the project as resources, timing, project phases, and rates/costs change.

See Figure 8 for an excerpt of the JBH Project Staffing Plan.

JB Hair Care Staffing Plan
By Team (Initial Phase)

Role	Last Name	First Name	1/1/20XX 1/31/20XX	2/1/20XX 2/28/20XX	3/1/20XX 3/31/20XX	4/1/20XX 4/30/20XX	5/1/20XX 5/31/20XX	6/1/20XX 6/30/20XX	7/1/20XX 7/31/20XX	Total Hours	Current Rate	Org Budget	Notes
Program Manager	West	Serena	160	160	160	160	160	160	160	1120	$150	$168,000	
Project Manager	Alexander	Drey	160	160	160	160	160	160	160	1120	$120	$134,400	
Manager	Daniewy	Felix	160	160	160	160	160	160	160	1120	$75	$84,000	
Team Leader	Arnold	Trudy	160	160	160	160	160	160	160	1120	$55	$61,600	
Team Member	David	Andy	0	0	160	160	160	160	160	800	$45	$36,000	Andy David starts in March.
Team Member	Merris	Jordan	160	160	160	160	160	160	160	1120	$45	$50,400	
Team Member	Paul	Michelle	160	160	160	160	160	160	160	1120	$45	$50,400	
Off Shore Technical	Madox	Chester	0	0	160	160	160	160	160	800	$35	$28,000	Chester Maddox will not be avail until March.
										7280		$444,800	
Project Manager	Sullivan	Kim	160	160	160	160	160	160	160	1120	$120	$134,400	
Manager	Duncan	Sylvia	160	160	160	160	160	160	160	1120	$75	$84,000	
Team Leader	Faulkner	Iris	160	160	160	160	160	160	160	1120	$55	$61,600	
Team Member	Archer	Thomas	160	160	160	160	160	160	160	1120	$45	$50,400	
Team Member	Myers	Myrna	160	160	160	160	160	160	160	1120	$45	$50,400	
Team Member	Wilson	Carl	160	160	160	160	160	160	160	1120	$45	$50,400	
Team Member	Frankford	Gladys	160	160	160	160	160	160	160	1120	$45	$50,400	
										7840		$481,600	

Figure 8: JBH Project Staffing Plan

Chapter 4: Communications Meeting

urpose: Meet with the project team to develop and refine the organization chart, RACI chart (RACI stands for "Responsibility, Accountability, Consult and Inform"), status-reporting requirements, and project governance (issues, risks, change requests, and action items) processes. This meeting focuses on both the A (accountability and risk) and the L (leadership/communication) of the PASTELS project management elements.

- *Accountability and risk* must be properly documented and communicated to ensure all team members understand how communication flows, and their responsibilities within those communications. It also deals with understanding how to identify and document risks and other governance items in the project.

- *Leadership/communication* must be employed to make sure the team knows the methods and tools they must use to work together and achieve the project's objectives.

This Communications Meeting's purpose is to explain how communication should occur, and the appropriate method and frequency. At the meeting, a communications matrix should be presented that includes all team members as well as stakeholders of the project. This matrix provides a quick-reference snapshot of the communication tools used, what is communicated, to whom it should be communicated, the frequency of the communication, and the type of tool used (i.e., a meeting, an e-mail, a brainstorming session, a site visit, and so on). See Figure 9 for an example of the JBH Communications Matrix in the Communications Plan.

What	Who/Target	Purpose	When/Frequency	Type/Method(s)
Project Kick-Off	All management stakeholders*	• Communicate project objective, plans, timeline and roles/responsibilities.	• At Initiation for H/L Kickoff. • At Project Start Project Teams	• Kickoff Meeting
Communication Plan	• All project stakeholders	• Identify communication requirements • Communicate updates, status and/or, issues	• Weekly	• Via Email Post to project document repository
Team Meetings	• Project Teams Members	• Review deliverables, timeline, assignments, action items, risks, issues, questions and change requests.	• Weekly	• Team Meeting
Executive Sponsor Meetings	• H/L Sponsors • Program Manager • SMEs as needed	• Provide project status updates, discuss project concerns, resource changes, and issues.	• As needed. • Frequency may increase during execution.	• Meeting
Issue Escalation	• Project Sponsor • Executive Leadership • PMO • Stakeholders	• Review issues that need management attention	• Weekly • Or more frequently if Needed	• Special Meetings • Email Escalation
Change Mgt Process	• Project Sponsor • Executive Leadership • Change Review Board • PMO • Stakeholders	• Address changes to timeline, project scope or resources including impact assessments and mitigation planning	• Weekly • Or more frequently if Needed	• Weekly Management Meeting • Updates made to document repository • Email to keep everyone informed
Milestone and Phase Exit	• Project Sponsor • Executive Leadership • Change Review Board • PMO • Stakeholders	• Document lessons learned • Review milestone and phase accomplishments.	• End of milestones and phases	• Special Meetings • Milestone Reports • Phase end reports

Figure 9: JBH Communications Matrix

Conduct Communications Meeting

To conduct the JBH Communications Meeting, it is first necessary to understand the components of project governance and execution. Project governance consists of developing and establishing a formal model to identify and mitigate risks, identify and address problems/issues, identify and complete action items, and identify and address change requests. The Project Management Organization (PMO) resources (program manager and project managers), the business project leader, and the work stream leads, will be in attendance.

The project governance structure is vital to understanding how to properly oversee a project and effectively communicate changes, challenges and solutions. To effectively manage this on small, medium, or large projects, it is important to develop and implement a project communications plan. This plan includes a group of tools and processes that management as well as project team members have reviewed and agree on implementing in the project.

To effectively conduct this JBH Communications Meeting, the communications plan is developed with an executive summary. The executive summary is considered the overview of the document. It allows anyone to simply pick up the document and read, within a few paragraphs, the key points of effective project communication and status-reporting processes, and understand the basic processes governing issue/risk identification and mitigation. See Figure 10 for an example of the first page of the JBH Communications Plan Excerpt.

1.0 Executive Summary

This document was created to provide the project communication requirements for the CRM project that is focused on enhancing our customer experience and to provide for ease of use in doing business with JBH, This project will define the business model for all communications with our customers.

What: Communication Objectives
The key objectives of this Communication Plan are:
- To set priorities for the project
- To solicit support of the organizations stakeholders
- To provide details on the communications to all stakeholders
- To provide details for consistent vehicles that will be used throughout the project

Who: Target Profile
This communications media will be used to address all project communications to all stakeholders both internal and external.
What: Communication Tools
Communication tools that will be used for this project are detailed below:

Figure 10: JBH Communications Plan Excerpt

Within overall project communications, there are several tools the team can use to effectively communicate. These tools consist of the project organization chart, the RACI chart, the project status report, and the project governance log. These tools form the foundation of an effective communications structure.

Project Organization Chart

The project organization chart is a tool that is invaluable on a project. It gives everyone a quick, clear understanding of the reporting structure, the key departments, how the departments are organized, the stakeholders, and the team members. Refer back to Figure 7 for an example of the JBH Project Organization Chart.

This example chart communicates order, clear objectives, and structure. It can be used when a new person joins your team, to swiftly communicate the team's reporting structure and the high-level roles-and-responsibilities. However, this tool must be continually updated to ensure the information is correct. As your project evolves, you can progressively elaborate on this chart by adding people's names, key skills, start and end dates, and other changes to its elements.

RACI Chart

As mentioned previously, RACI stands for "responsibility, accountability, consult and inform." The RACI chart is a standard project-management communication tool used to clearly communicate roles and responsibilities on a project. The RACI chart uses the organization chart to further define the roles on a project, and then uses those roles to further clarify who is responsible, accountable, consulted, and informed. It can also be used to inform stakeholders of task responsibilities and accountability. See Figure 11 for an example of the JBH Project RACI Chart.

Team	Role	Last Name	First Name	Develop H/L Plan
IT	Project Manager	Kensa	Martin	R
IT	Manager	Dunlevy	Felix	C
IT	Team Leader	Arnold	Trudy	I
IT	Team Member	David	Andy	I
IT	Team Member	Morris	Jordan	I
IT	Team Member	Paul	Michelle	I
IT	Off Shore Technical	Madox	Chester	I
Marketing	Project Manager	Rothman	Joyce	R
Marketing	Manager	Duncan	Sylvia	C
Marketing	Team Leader	Faulkner	Iris	I
Marketing	Team Member	Archer	Thomas	I
Marketing	Team Member	Myers	Myrna	I
Marketing	Team Member	Wilson	Carl	I
Marketing	Team Member	Frankford	Gladys	I
Finance	Project Manager	Warner	Barbara	R
Finance	Manager	Hanover	Billy	C
Finance	Team Leader	Reamsey	Charlotte	I
Finance	Team Member	Peyton	Tyron	I
Finance	Team Member	Vu	Eron	I

Figure 11: JBH Project RACI Chart

A RACI should be developed and communicated in the communications plan as well as referenced in the various project governance meetings to ensure clear understanding of roles, responsibilities and expectations. It's important to update this chart, as roles and responsibilities change on the project.

Status Reporting

Status reporting is another fundamental tool detailed in the communication plan. This tool allows the project team to report on status of the project in an orderly, timely and efficient manner. See Figure 12 for an example of the JBH Project Status Report.

Figure 12: JBH Project Status Report

The details of the status report that must be outlined in the communications plan are frequency, format, and audience. Also, it must be clearly understood how the information will be used by management to provide oversight and support to the project team. Key components of the format for the status report, and its functions, are as follows:

- Relay current summary project status (including high-

level comments on the project)
- Highlight any outstanding major issues, risks and/or questions
- Recap all project milestones
- Relay accomplishments for the work stream for the week
- Convey next steps (tasks) for the following week
- Recap any potential budget impacts with special notes

Governance Log

Inherent in any communication plan is a method to identify risks and issues, and guidance on resolving those items on a daily basis. This section denotes the tool used (for example—SharePoint list, Excel spreadsheet, and other programs), the format, the method for how these items will be reviewed and analyzed, and to whom these items will be communicated on a regular basis.

The appropriate identification and mitigation process is key to ensuring the project team has an active voice in monitoring and governing their project. See Figure 13 for an example of the JBH Project Governance Log instruction sheet that defines each type of governance category.

Type	Definition	HIGH	MEDIUM	LOW
Change Requests	Changes that are being requested to the approved timeline, budget or scope of the project.	NA	NA	NA
Questions & Key Decisions	These are open items that must be address so that the work streams can continue to define intended deliverables or timeframes.	Potential risk to the JBH or it's customers	Potential risk to the established timeframes or project deliverables of the CRM implementation.	Potential risk to only one work stream without integration potential.
Action Items	These are activities that will need to be addressed by specific Work streams or individuals.	NA	NA	NA
Issues	This is an event that has occurred that could jeopardizing the project dates or quality of deliverable.	Potential risk to the JBH or it's customers	Potential risk to the established timeframes or project deliverables of the CRM implementation.	Potential risk to only one work stream without integration potential.
Risks	This is an event that has not happened, but has the potential to jeopardize the project dates and/or quality of scheduled deliverables.	Potential risk to the JBH or it's customers	Potential risk to the established timeframes or project deliverables of the CRM implementation.	Potential risk to only one work stream without integration potential.

Figure 13: JBH Project Governance Log

Governance Items

Based on the definitions of each governance category, it is important to note there are distinct differences between each, and that they are used at various times in the project.

Change Requests: Change requests can be identified by anyone on the project for reasons such as a configuration change, coding changes, resource changes, budget fluctuations, or schedule variances. Once these change requests are identified, they are documented and logged in the spreadsheet and sent for review to the change review board. The board then reviews the request, in accordance with all other requests, and approves or disapproves based on the priority and relative importance of the change to the project. See Figure 14 for an example of the JBH Change Request Log created for the project.

JBH Change Request Log

C-ID#	Originator	Work Stream	Closed	Date Opened	Follow-Up Date	Description	Reason	Owner	Mitigation Steps
C0001	Drey A.	IT	Open	1/03/20XX	1/11/20XX	Move data archive activities to February.	Resource not avaialble in to accomplish in January as previously planned.	Trudy A.	
C0002	Barbara E.	Finance	Open	1/03/20XX	1/11/20XX	Add CRM Management Consultant for Finance	Help to move up the timeline.	Billy H.	Train current personnel to alleviate additional need to add CRM.
C0003	Kim S.	Marketing	Open	1/03/20XX	1/18/20XX	Move forward with FRP for new vendor.	Existing vendor is in Chapter 11.	Sylvia O.	
C0004	Barbara E.	Finance	Open	1/03/20XX	1/18/20XX	Need three additional resources for January.	No one has experience.	Billy H.	Consider IT offshore resources to minimize budget impacts.
C0005	Phil W.	Human Resources	Open	1/03/20XX	1/18/20XX	Need offshore resource for January	IT offshore resource not available until after	Adrianna M.	
C0006	Phil W.	Human Resources	Open	1/03/20XX	1/18/20XX	Onboard new resource per staffing plan.	In staffing plan	Adrianna M.	
C0007	Ephram A.	Distribution	Open	1/03/20XX	1/25/20XX	Bring in alternate resource in May.	Tony will be on PTO.	Roland W.	
C0008	Drey A.	IT	Open	1/03/20XX	1/25/20XX	Request change in PO amount ($50K) for Hardware.	Hardware expenditure increased.	Trudy A.	Request additional bids for hardware expenses.

Figure 14: JBH Project Change Request Log

Questions & Key Decisions: Questions and key decisions can be identified by anyone on the project, to help communicate key logic or business decisions. If someone in the organization has a question, it is logged and assigned to the work stream responsible. Each entry has a due date and a point of contact to help facilitate communication. In terms of a key decision, all decisions that will affect the project or steady state need to be communicated at all levels. See Figure 15 for an example of the JBH Questions & Key Decisions logged for the project.

JBH Questions & Key Decisions Log

Q-ID#	Creator or Originator	Work Track	Status	Date Opened	Follow-Up Date	Question Description	Severity	Owner	Decision
Q0001	Drey A.	IT	Open	1/03/20XX	1/11/20XX	Who will negotiate network upgrade needed?	High	Trudy A.	Trudy and Drey yo meet and decide.
Q0002	Phil W.	Human Resources	Closed	1/03/20XX	1/18/20XX	Will the train-the-trainer sessions be held on site or off site?	High	Adrianna M.	KD: All training sessions to be held on site to keep costs down.
Q0003	Kim S.	Marketing	Open	1/03/20XX	1/18/20XX	When will new logo be completed?	Low	Sylvia D.	Three final options have been chosen. The final choice will be made at EOM workstream meeting.
Q0004	Phil W.	Human Resources	Open	1/03/20XX	1/18/20XX	Will offsite space be needed for interim resources?	High	Adrianna M.	TBD
Q0005	Phil W.	Human Resources	Deferred	1/03/20XX	1/18/20XX	Mid year review is during implementation. Do we want to push the dates to minimize conflicts?	High	Adrianna M.	Will determine date at end of 1st quarter.
Q0006	Drey A.	IT	Open	1/03/20XX	1/25/20XX	Will network printers be needed for offsite resources?	Low	Trudy A.	TBD
Q0007	Ephram A.	Distribution	Open	1/03/20XX	1/25/20XX	Fleet vehicles licenses are coming due? Renew by district? How to handle	High	Roland W.	Roland is investigating.
Q0008	Drey A.	IT	Open	1/03/20XX	1/25/20XX	Co-locate the network team before or after freeze?	Low	Trudy A.	Review pros and cons to decide.

Figure 15: JBH Project Questions & Key Decisions Log

Action Items: Action items are usually logged as a result of a team or group meeting. They are used to document next steps and follow-up items that need to be accomplished to continue to move the project forward. The facilitator in the meeting should identify action items, but the project manager is usually tasked with providing reminders and statuses. The action item has a due date and a point of contact to help facilitate resolution. See Figure 16 for an example of the JBH Action Items logged for the project.

JBH Action Items Log

A-ID#	Originator	Work Stream	Status	Date Opened	Follow-Up Date	Description	Owner	Escalate to PMO
A0001	Drey A.	IT	Open	1/03/20XX	1/11/20XX	Forward correspondence to the PMO to have the dates changed on the hardware delivery.	Trudy A.	PMO
A0002	Barbara E.	Finance	Open	1/03/20XX	1/11/20XX	Change work stream meeting to Thursday from Monday.	Billy H.	Team
A0003	Kim S.	Marketing	Open	1/03/20XX	1/18/20XX	Update collateral material to include new JBH logo.	Sylvia D.	Team
A0004	Barbara E.	Finance	Open	1/03/20XX	1/18/20XX	Send Finance requirements document to PMO.	Billy H.	PMO
A0005	Phil W.	Human Resources	Open	1/03/20XX	1/18/20XX	Schedule follow-up meeting to review budget constraints for offshore.	Adrianna M.	PMO
A0006	Barbara E.	Finance	Open	1/03/20XX	1/18/20XX	Send final dates for review meetings.	Billy H.	Team
A0007	Ephram A.	Distribution	Open	1/03/20XX	1/25/20XX	Review logistics worksheet and finalize before end of month.	Roland W.	Team
A0008	Drey A.	IT	Open	1/03/20XX	1/25/20XX	Confirm arrival date for test servers.	Trudy A.	Team

Figure 16: JBH Project Action Items

Issues: Issues are usually logged as part of a team or group meeting, but can also be logged at any time. These entries are used to document short or long-term problems that will affect the project. Each issue has a due date and a point of contact to help facilitate resolution. It also has a severity rating, which identifies the issue's priority, as well as a mitigation section that articulates the steps to resolve the issue in the most expedient manner. Issues can have a big impact on project success and need to be constantly communicated and resolved to ensure awareness and action. See Figure 17 for an example of the JBH Issues logged for the project.

JBH Issues Log

I-ID#	Creator	Work Stream	Status	Date Opened	Follow-Up Date	Description	Severity	Owner	Mitigation
I0001	Drey A.	IT	Open	1/03/20XX	1/11/20XX	Change in H/W could affect milestone date.	high	Trudy A.	IT to facilitate H/W choices before initiation is complete.
I0002	Barbara E.	Finance	Open	1/03/20XX	1/11/20XX	Is financial reporting for international offices in Scope?	low	Billy H.	Decision to be discussed in next executive leadership meeting.
I0003	Kim S.	Marketing	Open	1/03/20XX	1/18/20XX	Have not chosen org to create collateral material.	medium	Sylvia D.	Three finalists have been chosen.
I0004	Barbara E.	Finance	Open	1/03/20XX	1/18/20XX	What tools will we use for matrix simulations?	high	Billy H.	Billy H. is awaiting signoff which is expected next week.
I0005	Phil W.	Human Resources	Open	1/03/20XX	1/18/20XX	IT offshore resource not available until after February	high	Adrianna M.	AM is finalizing a replacement.
I0006	Barbara E.	Finance	Open	1/03/20XX	1/18/20XX	Financial reporting tool has not been approved by work stream.	high	Billy H.	Approval expected in next work stream meeting.
I0007	Ephram A.	Distribution	Open	1/03/20XX	1/25/20XX	Resolve calendar visibility for all locations.	high	Roland W.	Analyst assigned to fix.
I0008	Drey A.	IT	Open	1/03/20XX	1/25/20XX	Resolve network connectivity before execution begins.	low	Trudy A.	Solution to be implemented within the week.

Figure 17: JBH Project Issues

Risks: Risks are usually logged as part of a team or group meeting, but, similar to issues, can also be logged at any time. The entries are used to document potential short or long-term problems that will affect the project. The difference between a risk and an issue is that a risk is something that hasn't happened yet; an issue is something that is currently affecting the project.

In terms of resolution, the risk has a due date and a point of contact. It also has a severity and probability rating, which identifies the priority of the risk and the likelihood that the risk will occur.

Another aspect to the risk log is the mitigation section. This section documents the steps to resolve the risk in the most expedient manner. Risks are usually reviewed and resolved at the management level, and are noted and tracked in project planning to ensure the project stays on plan.

See Figure 18 for an example of the JBH Risks logged for the project.

JBH Risk Log

R-ID#	Originator	Work Track	Status	Date Opened	Follow-Up Date	Risk Item Description	Severity	Owner	Mitigation Steps	Probability ®%	Notes
R0001	Drey A.	IT	Open	1/03/20XX	1/11/20XX	All servers may not ship as originally planned	H	Trudy A.	Check alternate sources and/or expedite shipping	90%	There are 3 vendors that may be able to ship.
R0002	Barbara E.	Finance	Open	1/03/20XX	1/11/20XX	Revised forecast may not be final.	L	Billy H.	Setup meeting to get by-in for final numbers needed.	30%	Get on Sr. Mgt agenda to confirm.
R0003	Kim S.	Marketing	Open	1/03/20XX	1/18/20XX	Collateral material vendor filed for chapter 11	M	Sylvia D.	Contact secondary vendor for availability.	100%	There may also be another vendor on west cost that is available.
R0004	Barbara E.	Finance	Open	1/03/20XX	1/18/20XX	Budget input not received from all teams on due date.	M	Billy H.	Escalate to departments heads to get completed by EOW.	65%	HR, Distribution and Marketing not received. HR will be done today.
R0005	Phil W.	Human Resources	Open	1/03/20XX	1/18/20XX	Difficulty finding Finance resource replacement because of skillset required. May push timeline.	H	Adrienne M.	Engage more contract firms to locate skillset needed. Offer bonus.	50%	The skillset can be found from the preferred vendor list.
R0006	Barbara E.	Finance	Open	1/03/20XX	1/18/20XX	Finance resource not available until April. May push timeline.	H	Billy H.	Work with HR to locate resource with appropriate skillset.	40%	Phil has already been contacted.
R0007	Ephram A.	Distribution	Open	1/03/20XX	1/25/20XX	Trucking strike could affect east coast deliveries.	H	Roland W.	Determine alternate methods of transportation where available to minimize impact.	40%	Meeting set up to discuss.
R0008	Drey A.	IT	Open	1/03/20XX	1/25/20XX	New upgrade V5 available in April. Has features needed for international customers.	L	Trudy A.	Determine future release date to accommodate new features.	20%	Bypass on new release until Pilot is stabilized.

Figure 18: JBH Project Risks

Project governance is a key concern for all members of the project, and must be monitored and maintained constantly. This is the glue that holds the project together and enables risks and issues, as well as the other governance types, to be properly mitigated and resolved to help ensure the project's success.

Chapter 5: Procurement Meeting

P urpose: Meet with the Vendor Relations Office (VRO) to discuss the plan for resources (man, material, and machines/software).

The procurement meeting ensures the appropriate resources are planned and ready to work on the project as needed. It focuses on the E (expenses and effort) of the PASTELS project management elements. Project expenses must be planned and procured to ensure that appropriate resources are available to meet the project objectives.

Conduct Procurement Planning Meeting

To conduct the JBH procurement planning meeting, it is first necessary for the project manager to understand the components of procurement. The JBH procurement plan details the contracts used on the project, the vehicles used, the contractors used, and the terms of these agreements. It also details the procurement approval process, and how to successfully plan and procure services, hardware, and software in the organization. It lists the tools to use, the appropriate authorizations to have, and the identities of procurement officers in the company along with their spending authorization.

Each component of the procurement plan focuses on the following key areas:

- Resources (services): The resources identified in this plan include contract personnel necessary to fully execute the project's objectives. These personnel are used to supplement the JBH staff, to provide the necessary expertise to develop and design the Customer Relationship Management (CRM) software. For JBH, these resources include services from their offshore technical group to help with development; the HR consulting group for subject matter expertise; and the distribution consulting group for subject matter expertise. When identifying the resources needed to support the JBH CRM pilot program, the organization looked at the tasks necessary, the time associated and the skillsets needed, and then identified the appropriate contract personnel to support the project.
- Hardware: The hardware procurement depends on the findings of the JBH infrastructure assessment. This assessment identified the need to procure one server to support the pilot, a server that includes backup support services. Additional hardware

procurements will be needed if the pilot is a success and plans are implemented to deploy across the United States or internationally.

- Software: The software procurement was developed by the consulting team who won the services contract. This team helped develop the list of the CRM software as well as the supporting software and support services needed to implement the CRM pilot.

This procurement plan is important to truly understand how and when supplemental support will be available for the project. Contracts are developed and maintained in the Vendor Relations Office and updated as needs change throughout the project. See Figure 19 for an example of the JBH Project Procurement Plan Excerpt.

Introduction
The JBH project procurement management plan sets the procurement framework for the project. It will be used to manage the procurement for the duration of the project. The plan identifies everything that will be procured, and contracts needed on the project, and the approval process that will be used.

Procurement Management Approach
The PMO provides oversight and will work with each project work stream. The PM assigned to each work stream will document and report all procurement items. The PMO is responsible to coordinate with the purchasing department for final acquisition.

The following products and services will be acquired for use in the JBH project. The PMO will coordinate the process to have contacts reviewed by the legal department who will determine the contract type and subsequently coordinate the purchase with the internal purchasing department.

Description	Acquisition Date
Offshore Resources	XX-XX-XXXX
Software	XX-XX-XXXX
Hardware	XX-XX-XXXX

Contract Approval Process
All purchases will be reviewed and approved by the Change Review Board. The process will require measurement as outlined in pre-established policies and procedures for vendor management.

Procurement Plan Excerpt

Figure 19: JBH Project

All procurements identified in the procurement management plan must be coordinated with the purchasing department for final acquisition. The legal department will also review the contracts, to make sure they are in accordance with the procurement management plan and the company's legal guidelines. From a project management perspective, the program and project managers need to work with the Vendor Relations Office (VRO), to constantly monitor the contract to ensure the consultants are performing per the contractual obligations. If there is an issue, the program manager will work with the Vendor Relations Office to resolve it.

Chapter 6: Integration/Planning Meeting

P urpose: Meet with the project team to develop the overall processes for integration across all teams. These processes include identifying the teams needing integration, the level of integration necessary, and the process to identify, escalate, and resolve integration issues and concerns.

Integration and planning spans the project, and can be grouped in both the S (success) and the T (timelines) of the PASTELS project management elements. The *success* of a project often depends on how well integrated the team is and the various support functions. The *timelines* or project work plan is important, because it enables the team to understand the tasks needed to progress through the project and complete it successfully.

Conduct Integration Meeting

To conduct the JBH Integration Meeting, it is necessary for the team to understand why integration is critical to the project's success. Integration must look at all aspects of the project and determine the specific integrative components to ensure the project completes successfully, the stakeholder expectations are met, and the requirements are met. The interdependencies of a project are quite difficult to identify and maintain, so this meeting is important to identify components upfront to obtain a successful result.

Integration can be defined as where the processes of a project interact. For example, in the JBH project, processes such as cost/budget, schedule, and governance, all interact. If you are modifying a cost or budget item, you have to also review and analyze the schedule to make sure it hasn't been affected. If it has been affected, you have to make appropriate modifications to ensure the project documentation accurately reflects the true operations of the project. It can also be said that in this example, an existing risk might need to be reviewed and closed, or a new risk might need to be developed, analyzed and resolved. Integration occurs throughout all projects, and it is important to define these integration points and have a structured process to manage and maintain them.

To effectively conduct this JBH Integration Meeting, the subject matter should be divided in the following manner:

Project Charter

Definition: The most important item that needs to be discussed is the project charter. A project charter allows cross-team collaboration in terms of officially approving the project, as well as documenting high-level requirements that the stakeholders can agree on and understand. Before the project charter is developed, the JBH executive leadership assigns a program manager to participate in the project-charter creation, so leadership can understand the project requirements and the stakeholder expectations from inception.

Stakeholders: The stakeholders invited to the JBH Integration Meeting consist of the program manager/project managers, business project leads, stakeholders (including business sponsor), and subject matter experts (SMEs). The project stakeholders are invited to ensure the charter is developed with everyone in mind, and that the appropriate expectations can be defined, agreed upon and documented. When the project charter is completed, it links the project to the overall strategy and operations of JBH.

Requirements: To understand the requirements of the project charter, the attendees of this meeting must have working knowledge of the project's statement of work (if already developed), any contracts already in place, the organizational structure, and the business sponsor(s) needs and business case.

Tools: The key tool used to develop the project charter is expert judgment. The charter must include clear and definitive language. High-level jargon that can be misinterpreted should be noted and removed. Consultants and experts from the JBH program management office should also ensure the document clearly articulates the purpose and objective of the project.

Template: To develop the JBH project charter, the program manager will fill in the template with key areas that were discussed above. Basic subject areas include identifying the key stakeholders and the business sponsor, the high-level requirements from each stakeholder, and risks, budget, schedule, and the project authorization to begin work. See Figure 20 for an example of the JBH Project Charter Title Page.

JBH Project Charter

Project Name: JBH CRM Pilot Project
Department: Sales & Marketing
Focus Area: This project is for a multinational company's start on a Customer Relationship Management (CRM) pilot project.
Product/Process: CRM System for 20,000 sales representatives

Prepared By

Document Owner(s)	Project/Organization Role
Kim Sullivan	Project Manager, PMO
Sylvia Duncan	Manager, Marketing
Leroy Sagwa	Executive Sponsor

Figure 20: JBH Project Charter Title Page

Project Management Plan

Definition: A project management plan is a central document to integration management. It organizes and presents how the project is planned, executed, monitored, controlled, and closed (*PMBOK Guide Fourth Edition*, 2008; page 48). If written correctly, it summarizes all the key integration documents in one format and allows the project team to clearly understand project processes and procedures.

Process: The process of developing a project management plan is highly iterative, and can be confusing if left unattended. The project management plan incorporates key plans that are important to the success of the project. Included in the plan are the following:

- Scope
- Project management processes (cost/budget, etc.)
- Detailed implementation of each project

management process
- Dependencies and interactions
- Work plan(s) to achieve the project objectives
- Change management plan, which identifies and manages the changes in the project
- Depending on the project (scope, complexity, etc.) other documents can be included in this plan as needed

Tools: The project management plan uses expert judgment to develop the plan and integrate the processes across the project. The experts are either within JBH or hired as external consultants. These resources ensure the processes are tailored appropriately for the project's complexity and scope.

Another key tool used in the project management plan is the project work plan. This plan contains the detailed tasks needed to achieve the objectives of the JBH Customer Relationship Management (CRM) pilot program. It includes critical information like milestones, task name, task duration, task start and end dates, task dependencies, and resources. The project manager can also show percentage complete, notes, comments, Gantt chart view, and other information. These views can be tailored depending upon the project team's communication needs.

The work plan or schedule is the heartbeat of the project, for project managers as well as the project team. It sets the pace of the project, facilitates identification of risks and issues, provides clear direction to the team on daily work effort, and enables communication from the project team to all stakeholders. It's imperative to keep the work plan up to date. Usually, it is updated multiple times, anywhere from daily to weekly. The frequency depends on how often the project's scope, milestones, tasks, dependencies, and/or resources change. See Figure 21 for an example of a JBH Work Plan Excerpt.

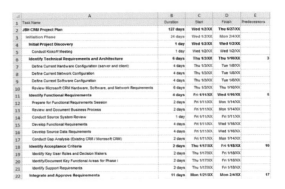

	A	B	C	D	E
1	Task Name	Duration	Start	Finish	Predecessors
2	JBH CRM Project Plan	127 days	Wed 1/2/XX	Thu 6/27/XX	
3	Initiation Phase	24 days	Wed 1/2/XX	Mon 2/4/XX	
4	Initial Project Discovery	1 day	Wed 1/2/XX	Wed 1/2/XX	
5	Conduct Kickoff Meeting	1 day	Wed 1/2/XX	Wed 1/2/XX	
6	Identify Technical Requirements and Architecture	6 days	Thu 1/3/XX	Thu 1/10/XX	3
7	Define Current Hardware Configuration (server and client)	4 days	Thu 1/3/XX	Tue 1/8/XX	
8	Define Current Network Configuration	4 days	Thu 1/3/XX	Tue 1/8/XX	
9	Define Current Software Configuration	4 days	Thu 1/3/XX	Tue 1/8/XX	
10	Review Microsoft CRM Hardware, Software, and Network Requirements	6 days	Thu 1/3/XX	Thu 1/10/XX	
11	Identify Functional Requirements	4 days	Fri 1/11/XX	Wed 1/16/XX	6
12	Prepare for Functional Requirements Session	2 days	Fri 1/11/XX	Mon 1/14/XX	
13	Review and Document Business Process	2 days	Fri 1/11/XX	Mon 1/14/XX	
14	Conduct Source System Review	1 day	Fri 1/11/XX	Fri 1/11/XX	
15	Develop Functional Requirements	4 days	Fri 1/11/XX	Wed 1/16/XX	
16	Develop Source Data Requirements	4 days	Fri 1/11/XX	Wed 1/16/XX	
17	Conduct Gap Analysis (Existing CRM / Microsoft CRM)	2 days	Fri 1/11/XX	Mon 1/14/XX	
18	Identify Acceptance Criteria	2 days	Thu 1/17/XX	Fri 1/18/XX	10
19	Identify Key User Roles and Decision Makers	2 days	Thu 1/17/XX	Fri 1/18/XX	
20	Identify/Document Key Functional Areas for Phase I	2 days	Thu 1/17/XX	Fri 1/18/XX	
21	Identify Support Requirements	2 days	Thu 1/17/XX	Fri 1/18/XX	
22	Integrate and Approve Requirements	11 days	Mon 1/21/XX	Mon 2/4/XX	17

Figure 21: JBH Work Plan

In terms of the software used to support the creation and maintenance of the work plan, there are many products to choose from. Some of the basic tools consist of spreadsheets, project planning programs, and collaboration software. These tools are developed for the Web, for PC and Mac users, and for smartphone and tablet PC users.

Perform Integrated Change Control

Definition: Entering, reviewing, assessing, analyzing, and monitoring changes to the program deliverables and processes is defined as integrated change control. Change control is a key process in integration management, and should be properly planned and executed with the appropriate tools and stakeholders. Change control should be managed at the executive leadership level (or at a lower level, depending upon the scope and complexity of the project) and the results of these changes should be monitored for effectiveness. Each change should be summarized to ensure all stakeholders understand how it affects the project as a whole as well as individually.

Process: The process of performing integrated change management can be exceedingly complex, but for JBH it consists of some basic rules.

- Rule #1: the executive leadership will provide support and guidance to all changes affecting scope, cost or schedule.
- Rule #2: the project management office will provide dashboard/status reporting for all changes.
- Rule #3: the business sponsor will provide support and alignment to all strategic directional changes.
- Rule #4: the business project leads will ensure alignment of process changes across the work streams.
- Rule #5: the work stream team members need to identify and document issues, change requests, risks, and key decisions. The change requests must be documented in the change management log. All governance items must be communicated immediately to all levels of the organization.

Template: To develop the change management log at JBH, the team must identify the information that is required for each change, identify the tool they will use to log the changes, identify the stakeholders who will serve on the change control board, identify how often the board meets to respond to project changes, and identify the change control procedures in case there is a disagreement in terms of the voting. Additionally, to support the change management log, there must be a process put in place to audit the effectiveness of the changes and ensure the project documentation is updated and the changes are being properly communicated to the project team. Refer back to Figure 14 for an example of the JBH Project Change Request Log.

Chapter 7: Quality Meeting

P urpose: Meet with the project team to develop the overall processes for quality planning and management.

These processes include identifying the levels of quality expected from the project and the means of assessing and improving quality in the project deliverables. The purpose of this meeting spans the project, and can be grouped in the S (success) of the PASTELS project management elements. Quality is key to any project, and must be intrinsic in both your tasks and your deliverables.

Conduct Quality Meeting

To conduct the JBH quality meeting, it's first necessary to understand the components of quality management. Quality management consists of identifying and documenting the project's quality policies, objectives, and responsibilities. Most quality management programs include three components: 1) Plan Quality, 2) Perform Quality Assurance, and 3) Perform Quality Control (*PMBOK® Guide Fourth Edition*, 2008; page 189).

Companies often overlook quality management, and the importance of the processes and procedures within. The reasoning behind this is found in the difficulty of identifying and then agreeing on acceptable levels of quality, as well as in quantifying the procedures for audit and control. Even though instilling quality in the project is an exceedingly time-consuming exercise, it's worth its weight in gold. A good quality implementation must ensure the project deliverables are not only complete, but are correct. Simple to say, hard to do.

To effectively conduct this JBH quality meeting, the subject matter should be broken up into three areas.

Plan Quality

Definition: The first item that needs to be discussed is how to plan quality. Planning quality makes sure this meeting is successful, and that the overall quality management processes will be implemented appropriately. Planning quality consists of developing processes and procedures to identify quality requirements or standards (*PMBOK Guide Fourth Edition*, 2008; page 189). It also consists of identifying how the project is going to comply with these quality requirements once developed.

Stakeholders: The stakeholders invited to the JBH quality meeting consist of the business sponsor, the business project leader, the program/project managers, and the work stream leads. These stakeholders were invited to ensure the key people involved in understanding the scope and requirements of the project are responsible for leading the teams in developing the quality plan. This ensures the policies and procedures developed are actually universally understood, and implemented from the top down.

Requirements: To understand the requirements of the quality plan, the attendees of this meeting must have a good understanding of the project's scope statement, the work breakdown structure, the cost and schedule baselines, and the risks and issues identified in the project governance documentation. This understanding is imperative to effectively develop quality requirements that are considerate of various project factors. As the project progresses and the project factors change, these quality requirements will need to be reviewed and updated for relevancy and adequacy.

Tools: There are many tools used to develop the quality requirements for a project. The tools that JBH uses are industry-standard cost-benefit analysis and benchmarking tools (*PMBOK Guide Fourth Edition*, 2008; page 195). The project team uses a cost-benefit analysis to understand the costs and benefits of implementing a quality program. This analysis allows the team to develop a business case for each quality requirement. In turn, this business case helps the team discern the cost of the quality process versus the actual expected benefit of the functionality. Another great tool used by JBH is benchmarking. Benchmarking allows the project team to apply best practices from similar projects, generate ideas for improvement, and give the team a basis for appropriate quality performance measurements.

Perform Quality Assurance

Definition: There are many schools of thought on how to perform effective quality assurance. In the simplest definition, quality assurance documents the processes to audit the quality requirements and determines how to review the resulting quality measures. This review will help to ensure the quality standards that were developed during quality planning are in compliance (*PMBOK® Guide Fourth Edition*, 2008; page 201).

Process: The process of defining and executing quality assurance enables the team to constantly look at how to improve the project. The management team developing the quality assurance processes must review the project management plan, project work in progress, project documents, and the change control results, to audit the appropriate processes and ensure these processes meet the quality standards identified in the quality plan. The management team will accomplish this through quality audits. These audits are structured and usually independent, and focus on identifying best practices, problems or shortcomings, and appropriate improvement procedures, to get the project activity back on track. The audit also helps define lessons learned that can be shared and communicated throughout the company (*PMBOK® Guide Fourth Edition, 2008*; page 204). Quality audits are a great way to confirm the implementation of a change request.

Tools: JBH quality assurance uses the process analysis tool as a major way to ensure a thorough quality review. The process analysis tool enables the audit team to flowchart each process and identify bottlenecks, constraints, and compliance with established standards. To complete the process analysis, the audit team will conduct a root-cause analysis to ensure that symptoms and problems are not confused (*PMBOK® Guide Fourth Edition*, 2008; page 204).

Perform Quality Control

Definition: Quality control consists of monitoring and recording results of project quality activities, to access performance and corrective measures (*PMBOK® Guide Fourth Edition*, 2008; page 206). This process identifies quality activities of poor quality and the recommended action to improve. The quality control processes will feed directly into the quality assurance processes.

Process: The process of performing quality control lies in using effective tools such as cause-and-effect diagrams, control charts, Pareto charts, scatter diagrams, and inspection. These tools attempt to analyze the data from the monitoring of the quality processes involved to improve the overall execution of the program. This analysis gives management keen insight into the true problems by statistically reviewing data, charting processes, and asking "Why?" and "How?" until a true problem is identified and analyzed (*PMBOK® Guide Fourth Edition*, 2008; page 208, 213). Inspection is a tool widely used in JBH processes. This tool provides detailed review (peer and audit-based) of the deliverables, and not only identifies deliverables that didn't meet quality standards but also deliverables that did. These best-practice examples can provide additional clarity to the project team on expected levels of quality. These examples can also become the basis of training exercises and programs.

Template: To develop the quality control inspection processes at JBH, the team must fully understand the deliverables in question and the established quality measurements/metrics associated with each deliverable, and conduct the assessment in a manner that doesn't interfere with established project activities. This inspection process starts with a review of the specific deliverable, development of the criteria of review based on the quality standards, the rating of the deliverable, detailed comments on the findings, a corrective action plan on how to correct this deliverable, as well as appropriate training to improve the quality of all deliverables. This inspection process should be conducted at specific gates in the project, and should include full participation from the project team and its leadership.

See Figure 22 for an example of a JBH Quality Inspection Graph/Chart. This graph shows the inspection results during the testing phase of the JBH Customer Relationship Management (CRM) project. These results depict how quality has been assessed during each iteration of testing, and how the level of quality (gauged by errors detected) is declining throughout the iterations. Analyzing this data can lead to a better understanding of where errors occur and how often, and where to focus additional resources to improve testing in future iterations.

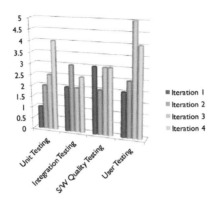

Figure 22: JBH Quality Inspection Graph/Chart

63

Chapter 8: Kickoff Meeting

P urpose: Meet with the project team and other stakeholders to kick off the Customer Relationship Management (CRM) pilot program. The meeting will introduce the scope, team organization, high-level timeline, and next steps for the project. See Figure 23 for an example of the JBH Kickoff Meeting Agenda.

Although this meeting doesn't have a separate PASTELS project management element, it can be grouped in the S (success) of the PASTELS project management elements. A kickoff meeting must be conducted with the appropriate people to ensure cross-team integration and collaboration, as well as to start all project team members on the same page. This meeting is a culmination of all the project meetings needed to start the project effectively.

Figure 23: JBH Kickoff Meeting Agenda

Conduct Project Kickoff Meeting

Before conducting the JBH Kickoff Meeting, it is very important to have held the various coordination meetings, with the purpose of getting the team on the same page. These meetings establish the project objectives and guidelines, as well as set the project budget and timeline. Once these key meetings have been held, the kickoff meeting serves as the final step to ensure senior leadership and the project team understands the objectives and expectations of the project. It's also important that each team member can clearly define project success, and measure it appropriately as the project progresses. This meeting also sets the coordination schedule, to make sure the project's status will continually be communicated and updated.

The key elements of a successful kickoff meeting are prior coordination at the team level, senior leadership buy-in, and creation of clear, consistent documentation for the meeting. This documentation outlines a project overview, team organization and communication, and project timeline. The next steps should also be identified and communicated, so there will be no misunderstanding of who will do what next to ensure the project is properly started and executed.

To effectively conduct this JBH Kickoff Meeting, each agenda item is presented in the following sections.

Project Overview & Approach

Create an overview of the project that includes key information, such as the purpose of the project, the expectations of the project, the key stakeholders/sponsoring organization, the start and end dates of the project, and the high-level methodology that will be used.

Team Organization

The stakeholders invited to the JBH Kickoff meeting consist of the executive steering committee, business sponsor, business project leader, program and project managers, and work stream leads. These stakeholders are invited to make sure they can clearly communicate the project expectations and scope, as well as the project's success metrics. During this part of the agenda, the project organizational chart and roles-and-responsibilities list is shown, to clearly articulate the project's structure. This communication is extremely important in the kickoff meeting.

Project Timeline

Another key component of the kickoff meeting is to clearly communicate the project timeline and associated risks. See Figure 24 for the JBH Customer Relationship Management Pilot High-Level Timeline.

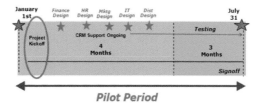

Figure 24: JBH CRM Pilot Timeline

It is important for all the affected department leads, the business leader, and the stakeholders, to understand the expectations around timing, and how each department is involved in helping the project meet that timeline. While communicating this timeline, it is imperative to discuss identified risks that could put the timeline in jeopardy, and the current mitigation plans in place to address the risks. And don't forget, if the timeline does shift during the project, the staffing plan, the budget, and the overall project management plan must be updated. Everyone must understand the impact of timeline shifts on the project and the budget from the very beginning. When changes are made, the change control process should be initiated to document variances from the approved scope. For further information about communication and timing, please see the communication plan in Chapter 4.

Besides understanding the agenda for the meeting, several other actions need to take place to make certain the kickoff meeting is conducted correctly. The following items discuss each aspect.

Roles and Responsibilities of the Meeting

To conduct the project kickoff, the project manager and the business project leader need to make sure attendees understand their roles and responsibilities and are properly prepared prior to the kickoff meeting. Please see the roles-and-responsibilities definition in Figure 4. These roles and responsibilities need to be documented as part of the kickoff meeting's agenda.

Kickoff Meeting Presentation

Template: To develop the JBH kickoff meeting presentation, the program manager will fill in the template with the key areas discussed above. Basic subject areas are the welcome, introduction of all participants, project overview, team organization, and timeline. Two additional slides should be included for next steps and questions.

When the attendees leave this meeting, they should be clear on the scope and objective of the project, their specific role and responsibility, how progress will be tracked, the overall timeline, implications of risks to the project and the process for identifying problems and improvements.

The kickoff meeting focuses the group on the project objective, project team, team communications and project plan, and conveys how to successfully move the project from conception to implementation.

Summary

A Week in the Life: Understanding the Role of a Project Manager has allowed you to take a sneak peek at the planning process a project manager goes through at the beginning of each project. As you've read through a typical business scenario, you might have already drawn parallels with your own project and identified preparation steps, key meetings to set up, as well as team members and upcoming interactions to plan.

As you think, *How can I get ready for this project?,* this book is for you. As you think, *What key things must I do to execute a successful project?,* this book is for you. As you think, *Who should I involve in the project and for what purposes?,* again, this book is for you. Simply put, this book is for you, as you prepare for and execute that critical first week(s), where you define scope and prepare the team for the upcoming rigors of the project. This week (or weeks), you set the baseline of the project plan, align key stakeholders, and ensure everyone on the team is ready and willing to accept the responsibilities of the project. Since this book takes you step-by-step through the planning process, it allows you to understand how and when to set up critical communications. In addition, through the use of our Meeting Basics Tips, we hope we have provided a great toolset to reference as you plan meetings and execute them.

Most of all, we hope you found this book informative, a quick read, a welcome reference, and most importantly, a timesaver as you progress through your various projects. We thank you for taking your time to read our book and welcome your feedback and input.

We wish you well in all that you do, and remember ... planning is fundamental, because it takes a plan to look into the future and obtain a project's possibilities.

Live long ... and plan!

Janice & Brenda

Appendices

Appendix 1 - Acronyms

Bottom Up/Top Down Estimating –

    Estimating duration / costs starting at the detailed summary level

Business Case – Return on Investment Analysis

CCB - Change Control Board

CR - Change Request

CRM - Customer Relationship Management

Expert Judgment – To use experts to provide knowledge

Go/No-Go - Milestone

JBH - JB Hair Care, LLC

Meeting Hijackers – People who take over the meeting and are not

    accomplishing the set objectives

Mitigation - To find a way to solve

PM – Project Manager / Program Manager

PMBOK - PM Book of Knowledge®

PMI - Project Management Institute®

PMO - Project Management Organization

Progressive Elaboration – To expand on a concept when more is learned

RACI - Responsibility, Accountability, Consult and Inform

SME - Subject Matter Expert

VIP - Very Important Person

Appendix 2 – List of Figures

Figure Number	Figure Description
Figure 1	Project Management Approach—Project PASTELS
Figure 2	JBH Project Management Week-in-the-Life
Figure 3	JBH Project Meeting Agenda
Figure 4	JBH Project Team Roles & Responsibilities
Figure 5	JBH WBS Example
Figure 6	JBH Program Budget
Figure 7	JBH Project Organization Chart
Figure 8	JBH Project Staffing Plan
Figure 9	JBH Communications Matrix
Figure 10	JBH Communications Plan Excerpt
Figure 11	JBH Project RACI Chart
Figure 12	JBH Project Status Report
Figure 13	JBH Project Governance Log
Figure 14	JBH Project Change Request Log
Figure 15	JBH Project Questions & Key Decisions
Figure 16	JBH Project Action Items
Figure 17	JBH Project Issues
Figure 18	JBH Project Risks
Figure 19	JBH Project Procurement Plan Excerpt
Figure 20	JBH Project Charter Title Page
Figure 21	JBH Work Plan
Figure 22	JBH Quality Inspection Graph/Chart
Figure 23	JBH Kickoff Meeting Agenda
Figure 24	JBH CRM Pilot Timeline

About the Authors

The authors bring their practical expertise to this Project Management "A Week in the Life" book to demystify project management, explain the project manager's role, and take you step-by-step through the setup and planning of a project.

Enjoy!

Janice Y. Rodgers, PMP

A California native, Janice Rodgers began her project management career as a software engineering officer in the US Air Force. She led many teams in the Air Force and used the PMI project management practices throughout her career. After she left the military, Janice went on to begin her consulting career, which focused on managing software development projects and executing program management principles and practices. More details can be found online at: http://www.linkedin.com/pub/janice-rodgers-pmp/0/796/692.

After using PMI practices for over ten years in her professional career, Janice decided to get her PMP certification to further enhance her expertise and job performance. Recently, Janice finished an SAP business-transformation project, where she led a sales and marketing team to implement SAP using PMI practices with the Advanced SAP methodology. Her expertise and practical applications of the PMI methodology is proven and extensive over her 20-year career.

Brenda K. Williams, PMP

An Ohio native, Brenda K. Williams began her project management career working for Fortune 500 companies and consulting firms in the field of project management. She received her PMP certification from PMI in 2005. Brenda managed software development projects and executed program management initiatives at major corporations throughout the United States throughout her 25-year career. More details can be found online at: www.linkedin.com/in/brendakwilliams.

Active in the community, Brenda is a past president of AWC (Association for Women in Computing), and member of both MPA (Microsoft Project Association) and PMI (Project Management Institute, Inc.). Brenda received the 2007 Woman of Excellence Award from the Federation of Houston Professional Women.

A WEEK in the Life
Understanding the Role of a Project Manager

You can visit us at
www.yourpmassistant.com
for FREE project templates
and other PM tools

~

Email us at
info@yourpmassistant.com

20151702R00047

Printed in Great Britain
by Amazon